Life Skills for Teen Girls Practical Skills Every Teen and Tween Should Know

Pretty Pickles

© Copyright 2023 - All Rights Reserved.

The content contained within this book may not be reproduced, duplicated or transmitted without direct written permission from the author or the publisher.
Under no circumstances will any blame or legal responsibility be held against the publisher, or author, for any damages, reparation, or monetary loss due to the information contained within this book, either directly or indirectly.

Legal Notice:

This book is copyright protected. It is only for personal use. You cannot amend, distribute, sell, use, quote or paraphrase any part, or the content within this book, without the consent of the author or publisher.

Disclaimer Notice:

Please note the information contained within this document is for educational and entertainment purposes only. All effort has been executed to present accurate, up-to-date, reliable, and complete information. No warranties of any kind are declared or implied. Readers acknowledge that the author is not engaged in the rendering of legal, financial, medical or professional advice. The content within this book has been derived from various sources. Please consult a licensed professional before attempting any techniques outlined in this book.

By reading this document, the reader agrees that under no circumstances is the author responsible for any losses, direct or indirect, that are incurred as a result of the use of the information contained within this document, including, but not limited to, errors, omissions, or inaccuracies.

TABLE OF CONTENTS

Introduction

Chapter 1: Communication Skills
Why Good Communication Skills Matter
The Art of Verbal and Non-Verbal Communication
The Importance of Active Listening
Finding Your Voice—Assertiveness in Communication
Navigating Conflict
Effective Communication in Relationships

Chapter 2: Financial Literacy
Money Matters—The Importance of Financial Literacy
Mastering Basic Money Management Skills
Budgeting 101—How to Save and Spend Wisely
Credit and Debt—Understanding the Risks and Rewards
Investing for Your Future—From Stocks to Crypto
Career Planning and Goal-Setting—How to Build a Successful Future

Chapter 3: Self-Care
The Importance of Self-Care
    Creating a Personalized Self-Care Routine
    Recommended Self-Care Products

Fueling Your Body—Nutrition and Exercise for a Healthy Lifestyle
    Why Nutrition is Key During the Teenage Years
    Exercise Guidelines for a Healthy Body and Mind
    Strength Training Versus Cardio—Which is Right for You?
    A Three-Day Meal Plan With Nutritious Recipes

The Power of Sleep—Tips for Restful Nights and Energetic Mornings
    Why Sleep Matters For Your Health
    How Much Sleep You Need to Feel Your Best
    Creating a Sleep-Friendly Environment

Stress Less—Strategies for Managing Stress and Anxiety
    Understanding the Effects of Stress on Your Body
    Different Types of Stress and How They Can Affect You
    Effective Strategies for Managing Stress

Taking Care of Your Mind—Maintaining Good Mental Health
Why Your Mental Health is Just as Important as Your Physical Health
Signs That You Should Talk to Someone About Your Mental Health
Tips for Taking Care of Your Mental Health

Chapter 4: Healthy Habits
Tips for Personal Hygiene and Grooming
Soak Up the Sun Safely
Navigating Sexual Health and Contraception
Strategies for Substance Abuse Prevention
First Aid and Emergency Preparedness Tips

Chapter 5: Personal Development
Setting Goals and Reflecting on Yourself
Time Management and Organizational Skills
Develop a Growth Mindset
Boosting Self-Esteem and Confidence
Discovering Your Passion and Purpose

Chapter 6: Household Skills
How to Cook - Recipes to Have in Your Repertoire
The Roast Chicken Dinner
Easy Roast Chicken Recipe
No Fuss Roast Veggies
Honey Dutch Carrots
Garlic Roast Potatoes
The No Cook Charcuterie Board
Chocolate Cake for Newbies
Tips on Creating Budget-Friendly Meals
How to Cook the Perfect Steak
How to Make the Perfect Salad Dressing
How to Host a Dinner Party

How to Do Laundry
How to Clean Your Home

Chapter 7: Safety and Survival Skills
Be street safe: going out with friends
How to change a flat tire
What to do if your car breaks down
What to do in an emergency if you don't have reception
What to do if you get stuck in the woods
What to do in a power outage?

Chapter 8: Social Skills
　How to make friends
　Friendship Etiquette
　Signs of a Healthy Relationship
　Dealing with peer pressure
　Avoiding gossip
　Stand Up to Bullies
　Respecting Differences
　How to Handle Criticism
　How to Make an Accept an Apology

Chapter 9: Digital Literacy
　Cyber safety

Conclusion

References

Introduction

It's so hard to be a teenager, incredibly difficult.
— Hugh Jackman

Well, I definitely don't blame Mr. Jackman for feeling that way because the teenage years are an awkward phase filled with hormonal changes, growth spurts, and constantly feeling that it's a battle between needing your parents to buy you whatever you need and wanting to be independent. It's no wonder that teens are often left feeling confused and overwhelmed. However, now you need not feel like you are walking through a minefield, because in this book we will be going through several strategies that will help you navigate through this tumultuous time easily.

From time management to basic budgeting—this book has everything you need to know at your age, so that a young woman like yourself can ace a job interview one day, and write a resume that no one can neglect, because let's face it, it can be pretty nerve-wracking to get that first job.

I know what you might be thinking after reading the title of the book; why do I even need life skills? Well, you need to trust me on this because I have been in your shoes before. Life skills can be your secret weapon, but only when you use them properly— they will make you more capable as a person and help you to become more independent.

But what are life skills anyway? In a sense, they are like superpowers, but the only difference is that you don't gain them overnight, but over a period of time. In simpler terms, they are a set of abilities that you need to learn in order to navigate through different phases of life smoothly and successfully. You can also call them the "building blocks of adulthood." Take it from me, being an adult is tough. You will have jobs to go to, bills to pay on time, and tons of responsibilities that you simply can't choose to ignore. However, when you have the right life skills in your toolbox, you will know how to handle everything like a boss!

Now, you might be wondering how this book is going to be of help when there is so much you've got to learn. Well, let me tell you. I've covered everything you need to know to face your teen life head-on. Whether you want to learn the skills required to negotiate your salary like a pro, or a simple day-to-day job like doing the laundry—you will be learning about everything, and it's not just the practical skills that we will talk about.

We will also dive into the social and emotional aspects of being a teenage girl. I will show you how you can handle that whirlwind of emotions that you are probably going through right now, while also standing up for yourself every time someone tries to bully you. Remember, let's also not put self-care in the backseat either.

So, go ahead and dive in. I can't wait to see all the amazing things you accomplish!

Chapter 1: Communication Skills

Communication—the human connection—is the key to personal and career success.
– Paul J. Meyer

Well, Mr. Meyer is definitely right about this one. Communication is a skill that has the power to make or break your relationships, be it professional or personal. As teens or tweens, you are at a very crucial stage of your lives, do you know why? Because right now, you are starting to learn how to express yourself or connect with others. That's why we are going to start our first chapter with communication skills. We will talk about everything, from active listening to conflict resolution.

Why Good Communication Skills Matter

You have probably heard people telling you numerous times that "communication is key." Guess what? This common saying is actually backed by science! According to multiple studies conducted in the past, it has been concluded that when a person has strong communication skills, it improves their overall mental health, helps them perform better in their careers, and they are also more likely to have healthy relationships (Huckle, 2019). Hence, in short, you can say that good communication skills are like a secret weapon that everyone should possess.

However, I understand that not everyone is born a natural communicator, and if that is the case with you, remember that it's not the end of the world. Communication is a learned skill, so the more you practice, the better you become. Do you know what the best part is? Being good at communication has nothing to do with being a smooth talker; in fact, conflict resolution, assertiveness, and active listening are all part of the package.

The Art of Verbal and Non-Verbal Communication

Whenever I talk about verbal and non-verbal communication, I am always reminded of peanut butter and jelly, because they just go together. Science says that a huge portion of communication that human beings engage in daily, is actually non-verbal. To be very specific, 93% of communication is non-verbal. This means that your body language, tone of voice, and facial expressions are extremely crucial whenever you are trying to convey your message to the other person (Spence, 2020).

So, what steps can you take to improve your non-verbal and verbal communication skills? Firstly, start by being more attentive to your body language. Are you avoiding eye contact, crossing your arms, or slouching? If yes, then you must try to make eye contact, maintain open body language, and always stand up straight, because this will show that you are interested and engaged in the conversation.

In the case of verbal communication, you will mostly have to work on being concise and clear. Whatever you do, don't use filler words like "um" and "like." It's always advisable to speak at a slower pace so that your message is clearer. You must also pay close attention to the tone of your voice because that is what determines whether you are conveying the right emotions.

If you feel overwhelmed by all this, don't worry; all you need is a little bit of practice, and soon my fellow teen and tween girls, you will all become experts at putting your message across—whether it's through your body language or your words.

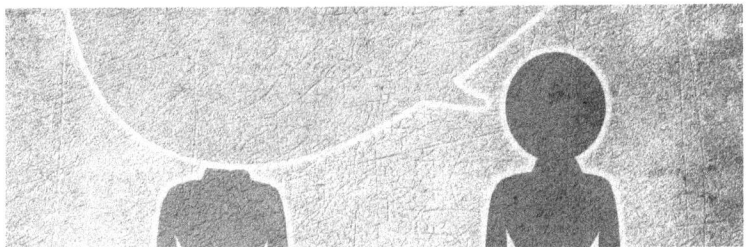

The Importance of Active Listening

Did you know that listening is not just about hearing the words someone is saying? It's about truly understanding the message and the emotions behind it. According to science, only about 25% of people actually listen effectively (Hanke, 2017). So, if you want to stand out from the crowd, it's time to become an active listener!

One of the best ways to become an active listener is to give your full attention to the person speaking. Put down your phone, look them in the eye, and avoid distractions. When they're finished speaking, summarize what they said and ask follow-up questions to show that you were listening, and to clarify any misunderstandings.

Another key aspect of active listening is to listen with an open mind. Avoid making assumptions or jumping to conclusions, instead, try to understand the other person's perspective. By doing so, you can build better relationships and become a more effective communicator.

So, let's start listening up! With a little bit of practice and a lot of patience, you can become an active listener and improve your relationships and communication skills.

Finding Your Voice—Assertiveness in Communication

As teen and tween girls, you're often taught to be polite, kind, and "not make waves." But sometimes, being assertive is the best way to get what we want and need. According to science, assertive communication can lead to better relationships, higher self-esteem, and less stress (Lonczak, 2020).

So, how can we become more assertive in our communication? One key tip is to practice saying "no" in a firm but polite way. For example, instead of saying "maybe" or "I'm not sure," try saying "no, thank you" or "I'm not comfortable with that." It might feel awkward at first, but with practice, it will become second nature.

Another important aspect of assertiveness is being clear and direct in your communication. Use "I" statements instead of "you" statements and avoid apologizing or making excuses for your feelings and opinions. Remember, you have the right to express yourself and be heard.

Navigating Conflict

Let's face it, conflict is a part of life and can be downright uncomfortable and stressful. But did you know that resolving conflicts can actually lead to stronger relationships and better communication skills? According to science, conflicts can be resolved in a healthy and effective way if we approach them with the right mindset and skills (Mirfattah, 2017).

One tip for navigating conflict is to take a break when emotions are running high. Take some time to cool down, reflect on the situation, and come back to the conversation with a level head. Another important tip is to listen actively and try to understand the other person's perspective, even if you don't agree with it.

It's also helpful to use "I" statements instead of "you" statements when expressing your feelings and opinions. Focus on specific behaviors or actions rather than attacking the character of a person as a whole. Lastly, always remember to treat the other person with respect and kindness, even in the midst of a disagreement.

So, my dear teen and tween girls, conflict doesn't have to be a scary thing. By using these tips and approaching conflicts with an open mind and a willingness to listen, we can navigate conflict in a healthy and productive way.

Effective Communication in Relationships

As teen and tween girls, you're all about forming connections and building relationships with those around you. Effective communication is therefore key to making those connections strong and long-lasting. According to science, good communication in relationships can lead to greater satisfaction, intimacy, and understanding (De Netto et al., 2021).

So, how can you improve your communication skills in relationships? One tip is to make an effort to really listen to the other person, and to show empathy for their feelings and experiences. It's also important to be open and honest about your own feelings and needs, and to communicate them in a respectful and non-judgmental way.

Another key aspect of effective communication in relationships is making time to connect and have meaningful conversations. Put down the phone, turn off the TV, and really focus on each other.

In conclusion, communication skills are an essential tool for navigating challenges in life and building strong relationships. From making friends and nailing job interviews, to resolving conflicts and expressing your emotions; effective communication can help you to achieve your goals and live more fulfilling lives.

Chapter 2: Financial Literacy

Money is only a tool. It will take you wherever you wish, but it will not replace you as the driver.
– Ayn Rand

Welcome to Chapter 2. In this chapter, we're going to dive into the world of financial literacy. Yes, I know, money talk isn't always the most exciting topic, but trust me, it's one of the most important skills you'll ever learn.

In this chapter, we'll cover everything from budgeting and saving, to investing and credit scores. So, grab a notebook and pen, and let's get started on becoming financially savvy young women.

Money Matters—The Importance of Financial Literacy

Money may not be able to buy happiness, but it sure can make life a lot easier. That's why financial literacy is such an important skill for you teen and tween girls to learn. Did you know that studies have shown that people who are financially literate are more likely to have greater wealth and financial security throughout their lives (Lusardi, 2019)? Well, it's true!

Financial literacy isn't just about making more money. It's also about learning how to manage the money you have and making it work for you. By mastering basic money management skills, like creating a budget and saving for the future, you can set yourself up for financial success.

So, let's start by taking a closer look at your spending habits and creating a budget that works for you. Don't forget to include savings goals, and also, make sure to stick to the plan! With a little discipline and patience, you can become a financially savvy young woman who is ready to take on the world.

Mastering Basic Money Management Skills

Managing money can be a really boring task, especially for beginners like you, but it's an essential skill to have if you want to be financially independent. Did you know that research has shown that people who are good at managing their money are less likely to experience financial stress (Ryu & Fan, 2022)? It's true. So, let's roll up our sleeves and get to work!

The first step is to create a budget that accounts for all your expenses, from rent to groceries, to entertainment. By tracking your spending and creating a plan for your money, you can make sure you are not overspending in any one area and have enough left over for savings. I will cover more on budgeting in the next section.

Another important part of money management is setting financial goals and working towards them. Whether it's saving for a car, or putting away money for college, having a clear goal in mind can help you stay motivated and focused on your finances.

Budgeting 101—How to Save and Spend Wisely

Did you know that creating a budget can actually give you more freedom and flexibility with your money? Yes, research has shown that people who budget are less likely to feel constrained by their finances and more likely to reach their financial goals (SDSU News Team, n.d.).

So, let's get to work on creating your budget. Start by tracking all your expenses, from that daily cup of coffee to your monthly phone bill. Hereafter, categorize your expenses into fixed costs (like the payments you have to make every month, for example, your tuition fees) and variable costs (like eating out or going shopping).

Next, set spending limits for each category based on your income and financial goals. Remember, it's important to prioritize your expenses and make sure you're saving enough for emergencies and future goals.

Finally, stick to your budget and adjust it as needed. Don't forget to celebrate your progress along the way! Through discipline and creativity, you can make your budget work for you and achieve financial success.

Credit and Debt—Understanding the Risks and Rewards

Hey there, let's talk about the "C" and "D" words—credit and debt. Don't worry, I won't judge you for that impulse purchase you made online last week (we've all been there). But it's important to understand the risks and rewards of using credit and accumulating debt.

Did you know that the average credit card debt in the US is over $6,000 (White, 2020)? This excludes student loans or other types of debt. But don't panic, there are ways to manage your credit to avoid falling into a debt trap.

One tip is to only use credit for purchases you can afford to pay off (in full) each month. This way, you can enjoy the rewards of building your credit score without accumulating interest charges. Speaking of rewards, make sure to take advantage of any cashback or reward programs offered by your credit card company.

If you do find yourself in debt, don't ignore it—ignoring debt won't make it go away—it'll only make it worse. Instead, create a plan to pay it off, such as the "snowball" method where you focus on paying off your smallest debts first in order to build momentum. Remember, having good credit can open doors for future opportunities, like getting approved for a mortgage or renting an apartment. It's important to use credit responsibly and try to avoid getting in over your head. So, let's be smart with our credit and keep that debt under control!

Investing for Your Future—From Stocks to Crypto

Hey there young investor! Are you ready to make your money work for you? It's never too early to start investing, and this section will teach you all about the different options that are available.

Let's start with the basics. Investing is all about putting your money into assets that will grow in value over time. Stocks, crypto, ETFs, and property, are all popular investment options. But before you dive in, it's essential to do your research and understand the risks and potential rewards.

For example, did you know that historically the stock market has returned an average of 10% annually (Hall, 2021)? While crypto is a newer and more volatile market, some investors have seen incredible returns in just a few years.

When it comes to investing, it's crucial to start small and diversify your portfolio. That means spreading your money across different types of investments to reduce risk. Remember, "investing is a long game", so be patient and don't let short-term fluctuations scare you.

If you're not sure where to start, consider talking to a financial advisor, or using a robo-advisor platform. These tools can help you build a personalized investment strategy based on your goals and risk tolerance.

Moreover, don't forget the power of self-education! There are countless resources available in books and online that can help you become a savvy investor. So go ahead, put your learning hat on, and start building your wealth for the future!

Career Planning and Goal-Setting—How to Build a Successful Future

Ready to talk about building your career and setting some goals? Let's do this!

Did you know that having a clear sense of direction in your career can lead to greater job satisfaction and overall happiness? According to research, people who set goals are more likely to achieve them than those who don't (Firmager, 2021). So, it's time to start setting some career goals!

First, figure out what you're passionate about and what skills you have. From there, research different careers that align with your interests and strengths. Don't be afraid to talk to professionals in the fields you're interested in and ask for their advice.

Next, set some short-term and long-term goals. Short-term goals can be things like improving your skills or getting an internship, while long-term goals can be landing your dream job or starting your own business.

Remember, it's important to be flexible and willing to adapt your goals as circumstances change. Also, don't forget to celebrate your accomplishments along the way!

Oh, and one more thing—don't be afraid to pursue side hustles or passion projects outside of your main career. These can bring in extra income and can also help you to develop new skills and make valuable connections.

So go forth and start building that successful future, one goal at a time!

I hope that by now you have a better understanding of the importance of financial literacy, and that you have learned some essential skills to help you manage your finances wisely.

With practice and patience, you can build the financial foundation you need to achieve your dreams and aspirations. So, keep learning and practicing these important skills, and don't forget to stay curious and explore new opportunities as they come your way.

Stay tuned for the next chapter where we'll dive into some essential life skills to maintain your physical and mental health.

Chapter 3: Self-Care

Self-care is giving the world the best of you, instead of what's left of you.
– Katie Reed

Welcome to Chapter 3! We'll be talking about the most important person in your life—YOU! That's right, it's time to focus on self-care. It may sound like a cliché, but it's true; you can't pour from an empty cup. That's why it's crucial to take care of yourself physically, mentally, and emotionally. In this chapter, we'll cover everything from developing healthy habits, to practicing mindfulness. Get ready to prioritize your well-being!

The Importance of Self-Care

I understand that with so much on your plate, you are quite the busy bee. Nonetheless, let's talk about something super important: self-care. It is said that "you can't pour from an empty cup." Well, that's what self-care is all about—taking care of yourself so that you can be your best self and take on the world!

Here's a scientific fact for you: Studies have shown that self-care practices can reduce stress, improve sleep quality, and even boost your immune system (Ayala et al., 2018). So, let's get into some examples of self-care routines you can try. How about taking a warm bath with your favorite bath bomb or face mask? Maybe you prefer to unwind by reading a book or taking a walk outside. Whatever it is that makes you feel relaxed and rejuvenated, make sure to schedule some "me time" every week.

Remember, self-care isn't selfish, it's necessary! Taking care of yourself is the foundation for living a happy and healthy life. So, go ahead and treat yourself!

Creating a Personalized Self-Care Routine

Creating a self-care routine can be as simple or as complicated as you want it to be. The important thing is that you make it a priority and stick to it.

There are so many things you can include in your self-care routine, from a relaxing bubble bath to journaling, or even just taking a few deep breaths. It's all about what works best for you and your individual needs.

Here are some tips to help you create your personalized self-care routine:

1. Identify your needs: Consider what makes you feel happy, relaxed, and rejuvenated, then make a list of activities or practices that you enjoy and that make you feel good.

2. Prioritize your routine: Schedule your self-care activities like you would any other important task—make it non-negotiable and commit to it.

3. Be flexible: Sometimes life can get in the way, and that's okay. Allow yourself the flexibility to adjust your routine as needed.

4. Try new things: Don't be afraid to experiment with new self-care practices. Who knows, you might find something that you absolutely love!

Recommended Self-Care Products

Are you looking for some amazing self-care products to add to your routine? Using the right self-care products can do wonders for your mental and physical health. For example, a face mask can help clear acne and exfoliate dead skin cells, while aromatherapy oils can help reduce anxiety and improve sleep quality.

When it comes to finding the right products for you, it's important to consider your skin type, allergies, and personal preferences. Some popular options include sheet masks, bath bombs, essential oils, and even weighted blankets!

So, go ahead and treat yourself to some self-care goodies. Your mind and body will thank you. Besides, who doesn't love a good excuse to pamper themselves?

Here's a pro tip: Check out reviews and ingredients before purchasing any product. Remember, what works for others may not necessarily work for you.

Fueling Your Body—Nutrition and Exercise for a Healthy Lifestyle

Let's talk about the fuel that keeps your body going: food! No, I'm not talking about the tasty junk food you love to snack on. I mean real, nutritious food that will keep your body healthy and strong. In this section, we'll cover everything from the importance of nutrition during your teenage years, to the right kind of exercise you need to stay fit and healthy. Get ready to learn about what you should put into your body and why, as well as how to get moving in a way that's both fun and beneficial. So put down that bag of chips, grab a glass of water instead, and let's get started!

Why Nutrition is Key During the Teenage Years

Do you know how important nutrition is for your body, especially during your teenage years? Well, let me drop some knowledge on you.

Your body is going through a lot of changes during this time, and it needs the right nutrients to keep up. Eating a balanced diet with plenty of fruits, vegetables, whole grains, and lean proteins, will give you the fuel you need to grow, develop, and stay healthy. Plus, it can improve your mood, cognitive function, and overall well-being.

Here's a tip: Try to limit processed foods, sugary drinks, and snacks which are high in salt and saturated fat. They may taste delicious, but they can leave you feeling sluggish and affect your long-term health (Naidoo, 2022). So, choose wisely when you're filling up your plate. Your body will thank you for it!

Exercise Guidelines for a Healthy Body and Mind

Hey there, my young fitness guru! Ready to learn some exercise tips to keep your body and mind in tip-top shape? It's not just about looking good in that new pair of jeans; it's about feeling good too!

Did you know that exercise helps to improve your mood by releasing endorphins (known as those happy hormones) (Mayo Clinic Staff, 2020)? Remember, it's not just about hitting the gym for hours; you can also get your exercise fix by doing something fun, like dancing or playing sports.

The American Heart Association (2018) recommends at least 60 minutes of moderate to vigorous physical activity each day for teenagers. Don't forget to combine strength training and cardio exercises for a well-rounded workout.

Here's a tip: Make it a habit to exercise at the same time every day, whether it's in the morning or after school, to help you stick to your routine. Also, don't forget to listen to your body and take rest days when you need it.

So, grab your favorite workout gear, put on some energizing music, and get moving! Your body and mind will thank you for it.

Strength Training Versus Cardio—Which is Right for You?

Are you confused about whether to hit the weights or go for a run? Well, fear not, because I've got your back!

Strength training and cardio both have their unique benefits, and the right choice for you depends on your goals and preferences. Strength training builds muscle and boosts your metabolism, while cardio improves your cardiovascular health and burns calories.

If you want to gain strength and tone your muscles, lifting weights is your go-to. But if you want to improve your endurance and burn fat, cardio is the way to go. Hey, why not do both? You can mix and match your workouts to keep things interesting and challenging.

Try alternating days of strength training with cardio or combine both in a single session. The possibilities are endless! Just remember to fuel your body with nutritious food and stay hydrated, no matter what type of exercise you choose.

A Three-Day Meal Plan With Nutritious Recipes

Alright my young foodies, let's talk about nutrition and meal planning! Don't worry, I won't force you to only eat salads and kale smoothies. In fact, a balanced diet should include a variety of foods that are both delicious and nutritious.
Here's a three-day meal plan that will keep you energized and satisfied:

Day 1

- ⇨ **Breakfast**: Greek yogurt with fresh berries and granola.
- ⇨ **Snack**: Apple slices with almond butter.
- ⇨ **Lunch**: Grilled chicken wrap with hummus, avocado, lettuce, and tomato.
- ⇨ **Snack**: Carrots and cucumber slices with hummus.
- ⇨ **Dinner**: Baked salmon with roasted sweet potatoes and broccoli.

Day 2

- ⇨ **Breakfast**: Whole grain toast with mashed avocado and a boiled egg.
- ⇨ **Snack**: Trail mix with nuts and dried fruit.
- ⇨ **Lunch**: Turkey and cheese sandwich on whole grain bread with carrot sticks.
- ⇨ **Snack**: Greek yogurt with honey and sliced banana.
- ⇨ **Dinner**: Turkey chili with mixed vegetables and brown rice.

Day 3

- ⇨ **Breakfast**: Oatmeal with sliced banana and honey.
- ⇨ **Snack**: Celery sticks with peanut butter.
- ⇨ **Lunch**: Tuna salad with mixed greens and cherry tomatoes.
- ⇨ **Snack**: Mango slices with lime juice.
- ⇨ **Dinner**: Grilled chicken with quinoa and mixed vegetables.

Remember, it's important to listen to your body and eat when you're hungry. Don't skip meals or restrict yourself too much. Don't forget to drink plenty of water to stay hydrated. Cheers to delicious and nutritious eating!

The Power of Sleep—Tips for Restful Nights and Energetic Mornings

Hey there sleepyhead! Are you having trouble getting enough shut-eye at night? Well, you're not alone. The importance of sleep cannot be overstated, and yet it's one of the most underrated aspects of self-care. As Arianna Huffington once said, "We sacrifice sleep in the name of productivity, but ironically, our loss of sleep, despite the extra hours we put in at work, adds up to more than eleven days of lost productivity per year per worker" (Schawbel, 2016).

Let's talk about how to get the most out of your slumber with tips for restful nights and energetic mornings. Trust me, you'll thank yourself in the morning!

Why Sleep Matters For Your Health

Hey there sleepyhead! Did you know that getting enough sleep is essential for your health? It's true! While staying up late might seem like a good idea when you're binge-watching your favorite show, it's not doing your body any favors. Sleep is when your body does its maintenance work—repairing tissues and boosting your immune system. Plus, sleep is crucial for your brain to process and consolidate new information (Fletcher, 2019). Lack of sleep has been linked to a whole host of problems, from mood swings to trouble concentrating. According to a study conducted in 2018, individuals who consistently sleep for less than seven hours per night have a greater likelihood of having a higher body mass index (BMI) and an increased risk of developing obesity compared to those who sleep longer (Cooper et al., 2018). So, make sure you prioritize your sleep, and don't skimp on those "Zzzs!"

The Amount of Sleep You Need to Feel Your Best

Well, how much sleep you need actually varies depending on your age. According to the American Academy of Sleep Medicine, kids between six to twelve years old should aim for nine to twelve hours of snooze time every day (Paruthi et al., 2016). As for teenagers aged 13 to 18 years old, they should try to get eight to ten hours of sleep per day (CDC, 2020).

Teens often have a bad reputation for staying up late, sleeping in, and feeling sleepy during class. However, teenage sleep patterns are just different from those of adults or younger kids.

During adolescence, the body's internal clock, also known as the circadian rhythm, shifts and tells teens to sleep later and wake up later. This shift is likely due to a hormone called melatonin, which is released later at night for teens than it is for kids and adults. So, it's harder for teens to fall asleep early (Gavin, 2019).

Teens are also dealing with a lot during this time of their lives. School demands are higher, and they're juggling extracurricular activities, part-time jobs, and spending time on social media. These distractions make it difficult to fall asleep at a reasonable hour.

On top of all that, school starts early which means that even if a teen falls asleep after midnight, they still have to wake up early for class. This can result in only six or seven hours of sleep a night, maybe even less. While it might not seem like a big deal, missing just a few hours of sleep each night can lead to a noticeable sleep deficit over time.

Creating a Sleep-Friendly Environment

Are you tired of tossing and turning all night long? Well, it's time to transform your bedroom into a sleep sanctuary! Here are some tips to help create a sleep-friendly environment:

1. First, it's essential to keep your bedroom cool, quiet, and dark. Your body temperature decreases when you sleep, so a cooler room can help you drift off more easily.

2. Use earplugs or a white noise machine to block out any distracting sounds and invest in blackout curtains or a sleep mask to keep your room as dark as possible.

3. Next, let's talk about your mattress and pillows. Make sure that your mattress is comfortable and supportive, and that your pillows are the right height for your sleeping position. If you're a side sleeper, a thicker pillow can help to keep your spine aligned, while a flatter pillow is better for back sleepers.

4. Lastly, avoid using electronics before bed, as the blue light they emit can interfere with your body's natural sleep cycle. Instead, try reading a book or practicing relaxation techniques like deep breathing or meditation.

So, go ahead and create your own sleep oasis, and wake up feeling refreshed and ready to tackle the day!

Stress Less—Strategies for Managing Stress and Anxiety

Feeling overwhelmed with school, extracurriculars, and everything else in between? Well, you're not alone! Stress is a normal part of life, but too much of it can be harmful to your physical and mental health. That's why it's important to have some strategies in place to help you manage stress and anxiety. In this section, we'll explore some ways to help you stress less, so that you can live your best life!

Understanding the Effects of Stress on Your Body

Hey there stressed-out teens! Let's talk about the big bad wolf of mental health: stress! Did you know that stress doesn't just affect your mood, but your body as well? Yup, those tension headaches and upset stomachs you get when you're feeling overwhelmed are all thanks to stress. But it's not all doom and gloom. Understanding the effects of stress is the first step to managing it.

So, here's the deal. When you're stressed, your body releases a hormone called cortisol, which can increase your heart rate and blood pressure. Over time, this can put a strain on your cardiovascular system, and increase your risk of developing health problems like heart disease and stroke (Mayo Clinic Staff, 2021).

There are several ways that stress can manifest in young adults:

- ■ **Irritability and anger:** Young adults may become snappy or argumentative when experiencing stress.
- ■ **Aches and pains:** Those struggling with stress may complain of increased headaches, muscle pains, and fatigue.
- ■ **Increased anxiety:** Stress can cause young adults to experience more anxiety than usual.
- ■ **Changes in eating habits:** Stress can lead to changes in appetite, with young adults either eating much more or less than usual.
- ■ **Neglecting responsibilities:** Young adults may neglect their chores, hobbies, or other responsibilities as a result of stress.
- ■ **Difficulty concentrating:** Stressed young adults may find it challenging to focus on their daily tasks as they worry about the cause of their stress.

Don't worry though, the ways to combat stress and its effects will be explored in this book.

Different Types of Stress and How They Can Affect You

Let's talk about stress. Did you know that not all stress is bad? That's right! Eustress, known as good stress, can actually motivate you to accomplish your goals. Too much stress, or distress; however, can wreak havoc on your body and mind (Lindberg, 2019).

There are three main types of stress: acute stress, episodic acute stress, and chronic stress. Acute stress is short-term and can happen in response to a challenging situation, like an exam or a presentation. Episodic acute stress is when acute stress happens frequently. Lastly, chronic stress is long-term and ongoing, like dealing with a difficult family situation, or living in a stressful environment (Ehrenfeld, 2018).

Different types of stress can affect you in different ways. Acute stress can cause your heart rate and blood pressure to rise, while chronic stress can lead to health problems like anxiety, depression, and high blood pressure. It's important to recognize the type of stress you're experiencing and manage it effectively.

Effective Strategies for Managing Stress

Stress is something that we all experience from time to time, but did you know that there are effective strategies for managing stress? Yes, it's true! Here are some tips to help you manage your stress:

- ▶ Exercise regularly: Exercise can help reduce stress by releasing endorphins, which are natural mood-boosters.
- ▶ Practice relaxation techniques: Techniques such as deep breathing, yoga, or meditation can help reduce stress and anxiety.
- ▶ Get enough sleep: Getting enough sleep is essential for managing stress. Aim for eight to nine hours of sleep each night.
- ▶ Talk to someone: Sometimes just talking to someone about your stress can help you feel better. This could be a friend, family member, or a therapist.
- ▶ Take breaks: It's important to take breaks throughout the day to give your mind and body a chance to rest.

By incorporating these strategies into your daily routine, you can better manage your stress and feel more in control of your life. Remember, stress is a normal part of life, but with the right tools, you can learn to manage it effectively.

Taking Care of Your Mind—Maintaining Good Mental Health

Well, hello there. It's time to take care of that beautiful brain of yours! In a world that can be stressful and overwhelming, it's important to prioritize your mental health. Taking care of your mind can be just as important as taking care of your body, and it's important to remember that the two are often interconnected. So, let's dive into some tips and tricks for maintaining good mental health, shall we?

Why Your Mental Health is Just as Important as Your Physical Health

Have you ever noticed how closely your body and mind are connected? It's pretty amazing! For example, physical pain can really affect how you feel emotionally, and it can impact your work and home life. On the other hand, when your mind is struggling with stress, anxiety, or depression, it can also take a toll on your body. The good news is that the reverse is true too—when you take care of one, it can help improve the other.

For example, individuals with mental health conditions tend to have a higher probability of experiencing sleep disorders, such as insomnia or sleep apnea. Insomnia can make it difficult to fall asleep or stay asleep, whereas sleep apnea can lead to breathing issues that result in frequent awakening. Additionally, those with mental health conditions have a higher likelihood of being smokers compared to those without such conditions. Moreover, smokers with mental health conditions tend to consume a greater quantity of cigarettes (Brennan, 2021).

Signs That You Should Talk to Someone About Your Mental Health

Here are some signs indicating that you should talk to someone about your mental health:

1. You feel sad or down for more than two weeks.
2. You have a hard time concentrating on schoolwork or other activities.
3. You feel irritable or angry all the time.
4. You're experiencing changes in appetite or sleep patterns.
5. You feel like you're not yourself or you don't enjoy the things you used to love.

Remember, it's okay to ask for help when you need it. Talk to a trusted adult or a mental health professional. They can help you to figure out the best way to manage your mental health and get you to feel like your best self again.

Tips for Taking Care of Your Mental Health

Here are some tips to help you take care of your mental health:

- **Establish a personal routine:** So, here's the deal buddy, your mental health is like a needy pet that requires some daily TLC. To keep that furry ball of emotions happy and healthy, you have to establish a routine that works for you. Maybe that means sweating it out with a workout or finding your inner Zen with meditation. You could even vent to a journal if that's your jam. Just do you, and make sure you're treating yourself like the VIP that you are.

- **Who is your support squad?** Life can be tough and sometimes you just need a little backup. Whether it's a BFF, therapist, mom, or wise old owl, having a go-to support system is key. You don't have to do it alone, just find your cheerleaders and let them have your back through the highs and lows. Remember, you're not a one-person show!

- **Remind yourself that you are not alone so embrace the power of connection:** It's time to drop the superhero act and embrace the fact that you can't do it all alone. Even Superman has the Justice League, right? So, when life throws curveballs at you, don't be shy to ask for a helping hand. Remember, your struggles and stress are what make you unique—and they don't have to define you. So, reach out to your trusted support system, whether it's your school club pals or your local community of friendly pandas. You'll be amazed at how much easier things become when you're not flying solo!

- **Start building that room for growth:** We all have those days where we feel like we're stuck in a rut, and nothing seems to go right. But instead of wallowing in self-pity or drowning yourself in a tub of ice cream (been there, done that), why not view each day as a chance to learn and grow?

Sure, life can be a real pain in the neck sometimes, but with a little mindset shift, you can turn those tough days into opportunities to become the best version of yourself. Besides, let's be real, who doesn't want to be the best version of themselves?

- **Take a breather:** In times of stress, it's essential to slow down and take a deep breath. But why settle for an ordinary breath when you can unleash your inner lion? That's right, it's time to channel your inner feline and let out a mighty roar on the exhale! Not only is it a fun way to relieve tension, but it's also a great way to get a little exercise in. So, the next time you're feeling overwhelmed, take a lion breath and let out a roar. Trust me, it'll make you feel better than a boring old deep breath ever could!

Remember, taking care of your mental health is a journey, and it's okay to take it one step at a time. Keep these tips in mind and don't forget to laugh and have fun along the way!

Chapter 4: Healthy Habits

Good habits formed at youth make all the difference.
— Aristotle

Welcome to Chapter 4. You are at an age where building healthy habits can have a significant impact on your future well-being. Developing healthy habits isn't about restriction or punishment. Instead, it's about creating a lifestyle that supports your physical and mental health, both now and in the future. In this chapter, we'll explore simple yet powerful habits that you can adopt to help you feel your best.

Tips for Personal Hygiene and Grooming

They say cleanliness is next to godliness, but who says you can't look cool while doing it? Maintaining personal hygiene and grooming is essential for not only looking good but also feeling good. Did you know that washing your hands frequently can prevent the spread of germs and illnesses? Or that brushing your teeth twice a day can keep your mouth fresh and healthy?

Here are some tips to help you maintain your personal hygiene and grooming:

- Take a shower or bath at least once a day.
- Use soap and shampoo to clean your body and hair.
- Brush your teeth twice a day and floss once a day.
- Wash your hands frequently, especially before eating or touching your face.
- Keep your nails clean and trimmed.
- Wear clean clothes and underwear every day.

By following these simple tips, you'll not only feel fresher and more confident, but you'll also be reducing your risk of getting sick. So, remember, clean is cool, and it's never too late to start practicing good personal hygiene and grooming habits.

Soak Up the Sun Safely

Hey there sun worshippers! While soaking up some vitamin D can be good for your mood, it's important to remember that too much sun exposure can damage your skin. That's where sunscreen comes in!

Did you know that the sun emits two types of harmful rays? Ultraviolet A (UVA) rays can prematurely age your skin and lead to wrinkles, while ultraviolet B (UVB) rays can cause sunburn and increase your risk of skin cancer (UV Radiation, 2019). So, it's important to use a sunscreen that offers broad-spectrum protection against both types of rays.

To protect your skin, you should apply sunscreen with a Sun Protection Factor (SPF) of 30 or higher every day, even when it's cloudy outside. Also, don't forget to reapply every two hours if you're swimming or sweating (Chien, n.d.).

Remember that sunscreen isn't your only defense against the sun. Wearing a hat, sunglasses, and lightweight clothing can also help. Just a tip for if you really want that sun-kissed look, try using a self-tanner instead of tanning beds or prolonged sun exposure.

Navigating Sexual Health and Contraception

It's important to know that having safe sex is crucial for your overall health and well-being. Did you know that nearly half of all sexually active teens will contract a sexually transmitted infection (STI) before the age of 25 (Sexually Transmitted Infections in Teens, 2019)?

So, let's talk about ways to protect yourself. One option is using condoms, which not only prevent pregnancy, but also reduce the risk of contracting STIs. Birth control pills are another effective method for preventing pregnancy, but they don't provide protection against STIs.

It's also important to get tested regularly for STIs, even if you don't have any symptoms. Many STIs have no symptoms at all, and early detection can make a huge difference in treatment and prevention.

Remember, it's your body and your choice. Make sure you are comfortable with any sexual activity that you engage in and don't feel pressured to do anything you're not ready for. Communication is key, so don't be afraid to have an open and honest conversation with your partner(s) about your boundaries and expectations.

Strategies for Substance Abuse Prevention

Drugs, alcohol, and other harmful substances can affect your health in many ways. Here are some quick facts to help you understand how substance abuse can be detrimental to your physical and mental health.

According to the National Institute on Drug Abuse (2020), substance abuse can lead to various health issues such as heart disease, stroke, liver damage, and even cancer. Substance abuse can also affect your mental health, causing problems like anxiety, depression, and memory loss. Not to mention that substance abuse can lead to addiction, making it hard to quit using a particular substance even if you want to.

So, how can you prevent substance abuse? Here are some tips to help you out:

1. Educate yourself: Learn about the harmful effects of substance abuse and the risks associated with using drugs and alcohol.

2. Stay away from peer pressure: Don't give in to peer pressure to try drugs or alcohol. Surround yourself with friends who make positive choices and support your healthy lifestyle.

3. Develop healthy coping mechanisms: Find healthy ways to cope with stress, such as exercise, meditation, or talking to a trusted friend or family member.

4. Seek help if needed: If you or someone you know is struggling with substance abuse, seek help from a professional. Treatment options are available and can help you to overcome addiction.

Remember, the most important thing is to take care of yourself and your health. Stay safe and stay away from harmful substances!

First Aid and Emergency Preparedness Tips

Ready to become a superhero? No, you won't have to wear spandex or a cape, but you will learn some life-saving skills in this section about first aid and emergency preparedness.

Did you know that approximately 60% of deaths related to emergencies occur because people didn't know what to do or didn't act in time (Hammett, 2017)? Don't be one of those people. It's important to be prepared for emergencies, and the best way to do that is to learn some first aid basics.

One essential skill is learning how to perform cardiopulmonary resuscitation (CPR) and the Heimlich maneuver. Knowing how to do these correctly could save someone's life.

You should also know what to do in different types of emergencies. For example, if someone is bleeding, you need to apply pressure to the wound to stop the bleeding. If someone is having a seizure, you should clear the area around them and help them stay calm until it passes.

It's also a good idea to have an emergency kit at home and in your car, with supplies like bandages, antiseptic, and medication. You never know when you might need it.

Finally, it's important to know when to call for help. If someone is experiencing chest pain, severe bleeding, or unconsciousness, call 911 immediately!

By learning these skills, you'll be better prepared to handle any emergency that comes your way. You may even be someone's hero someday.

Congratulations, you've made it through chapter 4! By now, you should have a good understanding of the importance of taking care of your body and your mind. From personal hygiene to sun safety, sexual health, and substance abuse prevention, you now have the tools to make informed decisions about your health and well-being. Remember, building healthy habits takes time and effort, but it's well worth it. By taking care of yourself, you'll be able to live life to the fullest and enjoy all the amazing experiences that come your way. Keep up the great work!

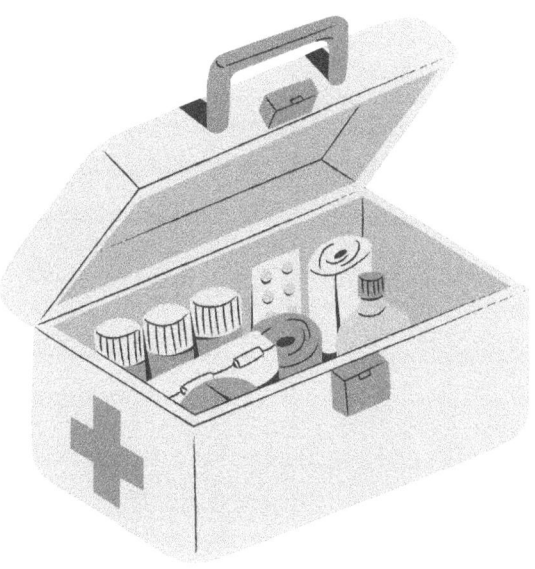

Chapter 5: Personal Development

Don't let yesterday take up too much of today.
– Will Rogers

This quote by Will Rogers perfectly sums up the importance of personal development. As a teen girl, you are constantly growing and changing, and it's essential to focus on your personal growth and well-being. Chapter 5 of this book is all about personal development. It's packed with tips and strategies to help you become the best version of yourself. From setting goals to building self-esteem, this chapter has everything you need to start your journey toward becoming the best possible you!

Setting Goals and Reflecting on Yourself

As Confucius once said, "The man who asks a question is a fool for a minute, the man who does not is a fool for life" (A Quote by Confucius, n.d.-a). So, let's not be foolish; let's talk about setting goals and reflecting on ourselves.

Goal setting is an essential life skill that helps you focus on what's important to you and motivates you to work towards achieving your aspirations. You can set goals for anything, from academic achievements to personal growth. Here's a scientific fact: According to a study, individuals who set specific, challenging goals perform better than those who set easy or vague goals (What Is Goal-Setting Theory?, 2013).

But setting a goal is just the beginning; it's equally important to reflect on yourself and your progress to achieve that goal. Self-reflection allows you to identify your strengths and weaknesses, adjust your approach, and stay on track.

Here are some tips to help you get started:

1. **Be specific when setting goals:** Set clear and specific goals that are achievable and measurable. For example, instead of saying, "I want to get better grades," say, "I want to raise my math grade from a B to an A."

2. **Make a plan:** Once you have your goal in mind, break it down into smaller, more manageable steps. This will help you stay organized and on track.

3. **Track your progress:** Keep a journal or use an app to track your progress. Seeing how far you've come can be a great motivator.

4. Celebrate your success: When you reach a milestone or achieve a goal, take the time to celebrate and reward yourself.

So, go ahead, set those goals, and reflect on yourself. You've got this!

Time Management and Organizational Skills

Alright, listen up! I know it's tough juggling school, extracurricular activities, a social life, and everything else in between. But fear not, for I am here to help you with time management and organizational skills that will make your life so much easier.

Did you know that studies have shown that effective time management skills can lead to reduced stress levels and improved academic performance (Khajeali et al., 2021)? It's true! By staying organized and planning out your day, you'll be able to tackle tasks more efficiently and have more time for the things you love.

Here are some tips to help you get started:

1. Use a planner or calendar to keep track of your schedule. Write down important dates, deadlines, and appointments so that you don't forget anything.

2. Break down big projects into smaller, more manageable tasks. This way, you won't feel overwhelmed, and you'll be able to focus on one thing at a time.

3. Prioritize your tasks based on importance and deadline. This will help you stay on track and make sure you don't miss anything important.

4. Minimize distractions. Put your phone away or turn off notifications while you're working on something important. It's tempting to check Instagram or TikTok every five minutes, but trust me, it's not worth it.

5. Take breaks! It's important to give your brain a rest every once in a while. Go for a walk, listen to music, or grab a snack. Just make sure you don't get too carried away and lose track of time.

By implementing these time management and organizational skills, you'll be well on your way to becoming a master of your schedule. Keep at it, and soon enough, you'll be able to handle anything life throws your way!

Develop a Growth Mindset

Having a growth mindset means believing that you can learn and improve through hard work and perseverance, rather than thinking that your abilities are fixed and unchangeable. Scientific studies have shown that individuals with a growth mindset are more likely to embrace challenges, persist through difficulties, and ultimately achieve their goals (Tao et al., 2022).

So, how can you develop a growth mindset? One way is to reframe challenges as opportunities for growth and learning. Instead of thinking, "I can't do this," try thinking, "This is a chance for me to learn something new." Another strategy is to focus on effort and progress rather than just the end result. Celebrate small victories along the way and recognize that mistakes are a natural part of the learning process.

Remember, developing a growth mindset takes time and practice, but it can be a powerful tool for achieving your goals and living a fulfilling life. So, believe in yourself and your ability to learn and grow, and see where it takes you!

Boosting Self-Esteem and Confidence

Ready to learn some tips to boost your self-esteem and confidence? Let's dive in.

Did you know that self-esteem and confidence are essential components of a healthy personality? When you have good self-esteem, you believe in yourself and your abilities, which can lead to positive outcomes. On the other hand, low self-esteem can cause negative feelings, including anxiety, stress, and depression.

So, how can you boost your self-esteem and confidence? First, it's essential to practice self-care and make time for activities that make you feel good about yourself. This could include hobbies, exercise, or spending time with friends and family.

You can also try positive affirmations. These are statements that you say to yourself to build self-confidence and motivation. For example, "I am capable of achieving my goals," "I am beautiful inside and out," or "I am worthy of love and respect."

Another great way to boost self-esteem is to challenge negative self-talk. Instead of believing the negative things you tell yourself, question them instead. Ask yourself, "Is this really true?" or "What evidence do I have to support this thought?"

Finally, don't be afraid to seek support from trusted family members, friends, or a mental health professional. They can provide encouragement, guidance, and help you develop a more positive outlook on yourself.

Remember, it's okay to struggle with self-esteem and confidence, and it takes time to build them up. But with practice and a positive mindset, you can achieve great things!

Discovering Your Passion and Purpose

Well done! You've made it to the final section of this book, and this is where we get deep and meaningful. As the wise Confucius once said, "Choose a job you love, and you will never have to work a day in your life" (A Quote by Confucius, n.d.-b). It's true! Finding your passion and purpose in life can bring you so much happiness and fulfillment.

Research has shown that when we engage in activities that align with our values and interests, it can boost our overall well-being and even improve our physical health (Souders, 2019). So, it's essential to take some time to explore and discover what really makes you tick.

Now, finding your passion might seem like a daunting task, but don't worry, I've got your back! Here are some tips to help you get started:

- Pay attention to what you enjoy doing: Whether it's writing, dancing, painting, or playing an instrument, take note of what you enjoy doing in your free time. These activities could give you clues as to what you're passionate about.

- Try new things: Don't be afraid to step out of your comfort zone and try new activities. You might discover a new hobby or an interest that you never knew you had!

- Reflect on your values: Think about the things that are important to you, like helping others, making a difference in the world, or being creative. These values can guide you toward a fulfilling career or hobby.

- Talk to people: Reach out to friends, family, or mentors who can offer guidance and support. Ask them how they discovered their passions and what steps they took to pursue them.

Don't put too much pressure on yourself to figure it out all at once. Take your time, enjoy the process, and most importantly, have fun!

Remember that personal growth is a lifelong journey, and it's okay to make mistakes along the way. Keep setting goals, stay organized, and maintain a growth mindset. Don't forget to take care of yourself and believe in yourself. Always remember that you have the power to create your own path and find your passion and purpose in life. Keep pushing yourself out of your comfort zone and try new things. You never know what amazing opportunities lie ahead. Keep growing, keep learning, and keep shining!

Chapter 6: Household Skills

"Having a clean home is not just about appearances; it is a sanctuary for the mind, a reflection of inner peace, and the foundation for a joyful life."
- Unknown

Whoever wrote that quote was wise. A cluttered home often leads to a cluttered mind.

You may not be ready to move out of your home yet but there are essential skills to know around the house that will come in so handy in case your parents are out of town or on a holiday with friends. Household skills can range from cleaning, doing laundry, maintaining your back yard, and cooking. This chapter is all about setting you up for success at home. Let's start with cooking as it's always good to have a small repertoire of dishes you know like the back of your hand.

How to Cook - Recipes to Have in Your Repertoire

The Roast Chicken Dinner

When it comes to handful of dishes you can master, you'll want a few classic recipes you know most will know and love, like the roast dinner. It's a classic dish with ingredients that are easy to source and it's the ultimate comfort food. There are plenty of variations on this classic dish you can find on the internet, here's my favourite.

What you'll need: 📖

- A whole chicken
- Seasoning like rosemary, oregano or thyme
- A bunch of carrots
- 1 kg of baby potatoes
- Brussel Sprouts
- Stuffing mix (optional)
- Gravy mix (optional)

Note: With chicken, you can typically find whole chickens with stuffing. If not, you can find stuffing mix at your local store.

Easy Roast Chicken Recipe

1. Start by preheating your oven to 425°F (220°C).
2. Season a whole chicken generously with olive oil, salt, pepper, and herbs. Rosemary or thyme go well with chicken.
3. From here, you can either insert the stuffing into the chicken, though most chefs prefer to cook the stuffing separately as it helps the chicken to cook more evenly.
4. Place the chicken on a roasting rack in a baking dish and roast for about 1 hour and 15 minutes, or until the internal temperature reaches 165°F (75°C).

No Fuss Roast Veggies

Tip: When roasting vegetables, always ensure that everything is cut to the same size. This will ensure they are all cooked evenly.

Honey Dutch Carrots

What you'll need:

1. Dutch carrots or baby carrots
2. Honey
3. Olive oil
4. Salt and Pepper
5. Rosemary or Thyme

How to cook them:

1. Preheat the oven to 400F (200C) and line a baking tray with baking paper
2. After washing them, trim the green leaves off
3. Coat the carrots in olive oil and drizzle with honey
4. Sprinkle herbs, salt and pepper
5. Leave them in the oven for 30 minutes, turning once at the 15-minute mark

Garlic Roast Potatoes

Tip: The secret to cooking crispy potatoes is to cook them on high heat

What you'll need:

1. 1kg of baby potatoes
2. Garlic (minced or finely chopped)
3. Olive oil
4. Herbs like rosemary or thyme

How to cook them: 🍽

1. Preheat the oven to 400F (200C)
2. Chop the potatoes into small cubes
3. Brush them over with olive oil and minced garlic
4. Season with salt and pepper
5. Top with rosemary and thyme

The No Cook Charcuterie Board

This isn't a recipe you can cook but it's so handy to have when you have friends or family over last minute and you want to serve something. A charcuterie board is a mixed platter of meat, cheeses and pickled vegetables or fruit. The ideal charcuterie board is a combination of sliced meats (think prosciutto, salami), hard cheeses (cheddar, gouda), crackers, pickled vegetables (pickles, pickled onion) or dried fruit. There are plenty of ideas on Pinterest you can copy. But here's one that's easy to source and assemble:

1. A serving platter (if you don't have one, a wooden chopping board will do)
2. Cheese knives
3. Mini ramekins or serving bowls for your pickled vegetables
4. 2 x Hard Cheese (cheddar and gouda)
5. 100g-200g of prosciutto
6. 100g -200g of salami
7. 100g-200g of ham
8. 1 x pack of water crackers
9. 1x pack of breadsticks of a baguette sliced
10. Fresh fruit like cherries, grapes or melon (you can also substitute with dried fruits like dates and apricots)
11. Pickled olives, onions or cucumbers

Chocolate Cake for Newbies

Once you've mastered a main and a starter, you'll need to find a perfect dessert. Knowing how to bake a chocolate cake comes in handy when you need to bring something to a birthday or a celebration…or just because.

What you need: 📖

1. A mixing bowl
2. Butter or spray oil
3. All-purpose flour
4. 1¾ cups of granulated sugar
5. ¾ cup of unsweetened cocoa powder
6. 1½ teaspoons of baking powder
7. 1½ teaspoons of baking soda
8. 1 teaspoon of salt
9. 2 large eggs
10. Milk
11. Vegetable oil
12. Vanilla extract

How to bake a chocolate cake: 🍴

1. Preheat your oven to 350°F (175°C)
2. Grease two 9-inch round cake pans with butter or spray oil
3. Mix all-purpose flour, granulated sugar, unsweetened cocoa powder, baking powder, baking soda, and salt.
4. In another bowl, whisk together eggs, milk, vegetable oil, and vanilla extract.
5. Stir 1 cup of boiling water to thin the batter
6. Pour the batter evenly into the prepared pans and bake for about 30-35 minutes or until a toothpick inserted into the center comes out clean.
7. Serve as is or add frosting and decorate

Tips on Creating Budget-Friendly Meals:

Life can get expensive and if you do the grocery shopping, you may notice that even cooking at home can be quite costly. Here are a few tips to help you save on meals.

1. Opt for ingredients that are in season as they tend to be most cost-effective
2. Plan your meals for the week ahead, that way you can buy ingredients in bulk and use them in multiple meals
3. Cook in large batches of soups, stews, or casseroles that can be portioned and frozen for future meals.
4. Consider growing your own food

General Cooking Tips:

1. Read the recipe before you start. Have all the cooking utensils and ingredients you need in your workbench before you start.
2. Chop your vegetables, measure your ingredients, and have everything organized and ready to go. This will make the cooking process more efficient and enjoyable.
3. Season and taste as you cook. Don't be light of the seasoning (salt and pepper).

How to Cook the Perfect Steak:

Cooking a steak to perfection is something to be proud of as it takes technique to master. Impress your friends and follow these steps to achieve a tender and juicy steak:

1. **Choose the right cut:** Different cuts of steak have different characteristics. Ribeye, New York strip, and filet mignon are popular choices. Look for steaks that have marbling, which adds flavor and tenderness.
2. **Season generously:** Season your steak with salt and pepper on both sides. Let it sit at room temperature for 20-30 minutes to allow the seasoning to penetrate the meat.
3. **Preheat your pan or grill:** Heat a cast-iron skillet or grill over high heat until it's smoking hot. This will ensure a good sear on the steak.
4. **Sear the steak:** Place the steak in the pan or on the grill and let it cook without moving for a few minutes. Flip it and cook for the same amount of time on the other side.
5. **Check for doneness:** Use an instant-read meat thermometer to check the internal temperature. For medium-rare, aim for 135°F (57°C). Remember to insert the thermometer into the thickest part of the steak without touching the bone.
6. **Let it rest:** Once the steak reaches the desired temperature, remove it from the heat and let it rest for 5-10 minutes. This allows the juices to redistribute throughout the meat, resulting in a more tender and flavorful steak.

How to Make the Perfect Salad Dressing:

Did you forget to pick up salad dressing in your shop? No worries. Here's a simple recipe that will go with most salads.

What you need:

1. Honey
2. Garlic
3. Olive oil
4. Lemon juice

1. Pour olive oil into a mixing bowl
2. Add in minced garlic
3. Add in a squeeze of a lemon
4. Balance with honey

How to Host a Dinner Party

Looking to have your girlfriends over for a fun night in? Here are a few tips to make it a success.

Dinner Party Preparation

Send your invite: Request RSVPs so you can plan your shop and cater to different dietary preferences or allergies. Paperless Post is a great option if you prefer digital invites.

Menu Planning: Aim for a well-rounded menu that includes appetizers, a main course, side dishes, and desserts. Offer vegetarian or vegan options if needed.

Simple Table Setting Tips:

1. Choose a theme and colour scheme. If you need ideas, white is classic. Start by covering the table with a tablecloth or placemats that match the theme or mood of the party. Choose colors and patterns that complement your dinnerware and decorations.

2. Place a dinner plate at the center of each setting, with a folded napkin on top. To the left of the plate, set a fork, and to the right, place a knife (blade facing inward) and a spoon. If serving bread, place a bread plate with a butter knife on the upper left side of the setting.

3. Set a water glass above the knife. Add additional glassware if you're offering other beverages such as mocktails.

4. Add a centerpiece or small decorations to the table to create a welcoming and festive atmosphere. Consider using fresh flowers, candles, or themed accents that complement your dinner party's style.

Example of a Dinner Party Menu:

Appetizer:

- Bruschetta with fresh tomatoes, basil, and balsamic glaze
- Assorted cheese and charcuterie board with crackers and bread

Main Course:

- Herb-roasted chicken with lemon and garlic
- Grilled salmon with a honey mustard glaze (vegetarian alternative: stuffed bell peppers)
- Sides: Roasted potatoes with rosemary and garlic, steamed asparagus with lemon butter

Salad:

- Mixed greens with cherry tomatoes, cucumbers, and a tangy vinaigrette dressing
- OR caprese salad

Dessert:

- Decadent chocolate mousse
- Fresh fruit platter

Beverages:

- Your own signature mocktail
- Sparkling water with lemon and lime slices
- Coffee and tea

How to Do Laundry

You've spent good money on your clothes, why not take care of them? If you are equipped with the knowledge to properly clean your clothes, they'll stay in top condition for longer
– you can even resell them on a marketplace like Ebay later on.

Let's start with the basics:

Know your clothing labels and fabrics:

Different fabrics need different care. Always read the care labels on your clothing and be mindful of the materials used. For example, most silk items will need to be dry cleaned and all wool items will need to be treated differently (or else they might shrink into a mini version of the item you had). If a label says dry clean only, it's best to follow them despite the dry-cleaning bill you might have to pay. Always follow the recommended washing, drying, and ironing instructions to avoid damaging your clothes.

Know how to treat stains:

There's nothing like that dreaded moment of discovering a stain on your favourite piece of clothing. Here's how you can get rid of them quick:

If treated early, you'll find that a stain may disappear when you treat it.

Apply a stain remover directly to the stained area and gently rub it in. You can use commercial stain removers or make your own by mixing ingredients like vinegar, baking soda, or dish soap with water. Let the pre-treatment sit for a few minutes before laundering the garment.

Don't have these items handy? Baby wipes or wet ones can work as an alternative for an on-the-spot treatment.

How to Do Your Own Laundry:

Sort it: Separate your laundry into different piles based on their care labels. For example, you may want to group delicate items e.g. bras and underwear in one pile, colorful activewear in one and your whites in another pile. It's important to wash whites separately as it'll keep them looking crisp white.

Prepare the machine:

Adjust the setting according to your load e.g. delicates, wools, deep rinse…etc.

Pour in your laundry detergent and fabric softener. If you have sensitive skin, you may want to opt for a natural alternative. They may not smell as fragrant as your typical laundry detergents but they can do the job just as well.

Load the machine: Place the laundry into the machine, but do not overload it. Overloading can prevent proper cleaning and rinsing. Your laundry machine will indicate the weight of the laundry it can support.

Tip: Avoid using hot water for delicate fabrics and cold water for heavily soiled items. Use a gentle cycle for delicate fabrics and a regular cycle for everyday clothing.

General Tips to Keep Your Clothes in Tip-Top Shape:

- Air-dry your clothes
- Over-drying can lead to shrinking, fading, and wrinkling. Where it's possible, let clothes dry in the sun to preserve the life of your items.
- Iron with care
- Use the appropriate heat setting on your iron based on the fabric type. For delicate fabrics, use a pressing cloth between the iron and delicate fabrics to prevent damage. Iron clothes when they are slightly damp for easier wrinkle removal.

Tip: Don't have an iron but need to freshen up a top quickly? Leave it in the shower, the steam will help remove the wrinkles.

Proper storage
Store your clothes in a clean, dry, and well-ventilated space. This is so important if you live in a wet or damp climate as it helps to prevent mold. Avoid hanging heavy items on delicate hangers, as they can cause stretching.

How to Clean Your Home

It may not be a life skill you need right now but it sure will come in handy. Whether you're new to cleaning or looking for some tips to improve your routine, here's a guide to help you effectively clean your home.

Cleaning Products to Have:

1. All-purpose cleaner: An all-purpose cleaner is versatile and can be used on various surfaces, such as countertops, appliances, and bathroom fixtures. It's a must-have.
2. Glass cleaner: For streak-free shine on mirrors, windows, and glass surfaces. Great for getting rid of those pesky fingerprints.
3. Disinfecting wipes or spray: Use these to help kill germs on commonly touched surfaces, such as doorknobs, light switches, and countertops.
4. Microfiber cloths: Microfiber cloths are excellent for dusting and cleaning surfaces. They are soft, non-abrasive, and trap dust effectively.
5. Baking soda and vinegar: These natural ingredients can be used to tackle tough stains, deodorize, and unclog drains.

A quick how-to on common spots you'll need to clean:

How to clean floors

1. Use a broom or vacuum cleaner to remove dust.
2. Depending on the type of flooring, you can mop or use a damp cloth to clean. For hard floors like tile or laminate, mix a suitable floor cleaner with water as per the product instructions. For carpets, consider using a carpet cleaner or steam cleaner.
3. Dip a mop or cloth into the cleaning solution, wring out excess liquid, and mop the floor in small sections, working your way across the room.
4. Allow the floor to air dry, or use a clean, dry mop or cloth to remove any excess moisture.

How to clean your shower doors

1. Wet the shower doors with warm water to loosen any soap scum or grime.
2. Grab your shower spray or prepare a cleaning solution by mixing equal parts white vinegar and water in a spray bottle.
3. Spray the solution onto the shower doors
4. Let the solution sit for a few minutes
5. Use a sponge or scrub brush to gently scrub the shower doors, working in circular motions.
6. Rinse the doors thoroughly with warm water

Note: If you are using harsh cleaning chemicals, ensure your windows are open and be sure to get fresh air in between cleaning.

How to clean a toilet

1. Put on gloves and gather the necessary cleaning supplies. You'll need a toilet brush, toilet cleaner, disinfecting spray and wipes
2. Apply toilet bowl cleaner to the inside of the toilet bowl, including under the rim.
3. Allow the cleaner to sit for a few minutes to break down stains and bacteria.
4. Scrub the inside of the toilet bowl using a toilet brush, focusing on the areas with stains.
5. Flush the toilet to rinse away the cleaner and debris.
6. For the exterior of the toilet, use a disinfectant cleaner and a clean cloth to wipe down all surfaces.
7. Finish by wiping the floor around the toilet with a damp cloth or disinfectant wipe to remove any splashes or spills.

Efficient Cleaning Techniques:

1. Start from the top: When cleaning a room, begin from the top and work your way down. Dust ceiling fans, light fixtures, and shelves before moving to lower surfaces.
2. Declutter before cleaning: Remove any clutter before you start. This allows you to clean surfaces thoroughly without obstacles.
3. Clean in sections: Divide larger areas, such as rooms or countertops, into smaller sections. Focus on one section at a time to ensure thorough cleaning.

Time-saving shortcuts: Optimize your cleaning routine with some time-saving tips. For example, spray cleaner on surfaces and let it sit for a few minutes before wiping to allow it to work more effectively.

Chapter 7: Safety and Survival Skills

Life can be unpredictable and emergencies can happen in the matter of seconds. We hope you'll never need to use the following but it's always best to be prepared, just in case. Use this guide as a reference to practical tips for various emergency situations, including being stranded without reception, getting stuck in the woods, and more. By acquiring essential survival skills, you can navigate challenging circumstances with confidence and resilience.

How to recognize an emergency

Immediate threat or danger: Assess your surroundings, are you or the people around you in a scenario where life, health, or safety is threatened? Emergencies often involve high-risk factors that require immediate attention. For example, this may include being in a concert or festival that has quickly become overcrowded or out of control.

Unusual or Unexpected Events: Look for events or circumstances that are out of the ordinary or unexpected. Sudden accidents, injuries, or the presence of a dangerous situation can indicate an emergency. For example, this could look like a distressed person who is acting out by screaming, yelling or exhibiting aggressive behavior.

Gut Feeling: Trust your instincts. If something feels wrong or gives you a sense of danger or urgency, it's important to take it seriously and assess the situation further.

Visible Signs of Distress: Look at those around you and look for signs of distress such as severe pain, unconsciousness, difficulty breathing, or profuse bleeding. If you're at a party and someone is unconscious, unable to breathe or in pain, call the police immediately in case there's been self-harm, alcohol poisoning or a drug overdose.

Don't be afraid to err on the side of caution even if people around you are telling you it's no big deal. When it comes to an emergency, calling emergency services can save a life.

Be street safe: going out with friends

You may have recently discovered the freedom of going out with friends without parental supervision – feels great doesn't it? Now that you have this new found freedom, it's best to be equipped with skills that will keep you safe while you're out and about – because not every person will have the best of intentions when it comes to your safety. Here are a few tips to keep in mind:

Be Aware of Your Surroundings: Pay attention to your surroundings, this includes cars and people around you. Avoid using your phone or wearing headphones that may limit your ability to notice potential dangers, especially at night.

Trust Your Intuition: Trust your gut instincts. If a person, place, or situation makes you feel uncomfortable, walk away and head to a crowded area.

Stick to Well-Lit and Populated Areas: Choose well-lit and populated routes, especially at night, even if it'll take you longer to get home.

Stay Connected: Always tell someone where you're going.

Buddy System: Travel with a friend or in groups. There is safety in numbers, and having someone with you can deter potential threats.

Maintain a Confident Posture: Stand tall, make eye contact, and be aware of your body language. This can help deter potential attackers who may target individuals who appear vulnerable.

Secure Your Valuables: Keep your phone, wallet, and bag out of sight. Avoid displaying expensive items that may attract unnecessary attention.

Know Emergency Contact Information: Memorize important emergency contact numbers, including local authorities and trusted individuals who can be reached in case of an emergency.

Be Cautious with Strangers: Be wary of strangers who approach you, no matter how friendly they may seem. If they try to convince you to go somewhere more secluded, politely decline and maintain a safe distance.

Learn Self-Defense: Consider taking self-defense classes to learn basic techniques that can help you protect yourself if faced with a threatening situation. These classes can provide valuable skills and boost your confidence.

How to change a flat tire

More essential safety and survival skills

Changing a flat tire is one of those useful skills that everyone should know, even if roadside assistance is available. Here's a step-by-step guide to help you change a flat tire:

Find a Safe Location: When you realize you have a flat tire, safely pull over to a well-lit and level area away from traffic. Engage your hazard lights and apply the parking brake.

Gather the Necessary Tools: Locate the spare tire, jack, lug wrench, and vehicle owner's manual. These tools are usually located in the trunk or under the floor mat of your vehicle.

Loosen the Lug Nuts: Using the lug wrench, loosen the lug nuts on the flat tire. Turn them counter clockwise, but do not remove them completely at this stage.

Position the Jack: Consult your owner's manual to locate the correct jack points for your vehicle. Place the jack securely under the designated point closest to the flat tire. Ensure the jack is resting on a firm and stable surface.

Lift the Vehicle: Use the jack handle to raise the vehicle until the flat tire is around 6 inches off the ground. Take care not to go beyond this height, as it may compromise stability.

Remove the Lug Nuts and Tire: Now, fully remove the lug nuts and set them aside in a safe place. Gently pull the flat tire straight towards you to remove it from the wheelbase.

Mount the Spare Tire: Align the spare tire with the wheelbase and slide it onto the hub. Push it all the way in until it is snug.

Secure the Lug Nuts: Begin threading the lug nuts by hand, ensuring they are tightened as much as possible. Then, use the lug wrench to tighten them further, rotating clockwise. Tighten them in a star or cross pattern to ensure even distribution.

Lower the Vehicle: Use the jack to carefully lower the vehicle until the spare tire touches the ground. Remove the jack and place it back in its storage location.

Tighten the Lug Nuts Again: Using the lug wrench, go around the wheel and tighten the lug nuts one final time, ensuring they are securely fastened.

Check the Tire Pressure: Use a tire pressure gauge to check the air pressure in the spare tire. Inflate it if necessary, following the recommended pressure indicated in your owner's manual.

Replace the Tools and Flat Tire: Put the flat tire, jack, and lug wrench back in the storage area of your vehicle. Ensure everything is secure and properly stowed.

Have the Flat Tire Repaired or Replaced: Remember that a spare tire is intended for temporary use only. Schedule a visit to a tire repair shop to either fix or replace the flat tire as soon as possible.

What to do if your car breaks down

Now that you may have a learner's permit or driver's license, you'll see to be prepared for emergencies that happen on the road, like your car breaking down. If it happens, stay calm and follow the steps below.:

1. Signal Your Distress: Signal to other drivers that you need assistance. Turn on your hazard lights to alert approaching vehicles.
2. Safely Move to the Side: If possible, steer your car to the shoulder of the road or a safe location away from traffic. Put your car in park and engage the parking brake.
3. Assess the Situation: Once you are in a safe spot, turn off the engine and locate the problem.
4. Use Warning Devices: Place reflective warning triangles or flares behind your vehicle to provide additional warning to other drivers. This is particularly important if you've broken down on a busy road or at night.
5. Call for Assistance: Use your mobile phone to call for help. Contact a trusted family member or friend to inform them of your situation and location. If needed, call roadside assistance or a towing service to request help. If you don't have a phone, some highways will have one for emergency purposes.
6. Stay Inside the Vehicle: It's generally safer to remain inside your car while waiting for help, especially if you're on a busy road. Keep the doors locked and only roll down the window slightly if someone approaches and you feel comfortable speaking with them.
7. Be Prepared with Essentials: Keep a roadside emergency kit in your vehicle, including items such as a flashlight, first aid kit, reflective vest, and water. These essentials can be helpful while waiting for assistance.

8. Communicate Clearly: When help arrives, clearly explain the situation and any symptoms or observations you've made about the car's condition. This information can assist the professionals in diagnosing and resolving the issue.
9. Follow Professional Advice: Listen to the advice given by the roadside assistance or towing service personnel. They have experience in handling breakdowns and will guide you on the best course of action.
10. Arrange for Repairs: Once your car is safely towed to a repair facility, consult with the mechanics to assess the necessary repairs and estimated costs. Be sure to obtain all relevant information, including their contact details and expected completion time.

What to do in an emergency if you don't have reception

It's easy to rely on wi-fi when it's so easily accessible but what happens if you're caught in an emergency without reception? Here are some tips:

Look for Alternatives: Check if you can connect to a Wi-Fi network nearby to get help. Or, try to find a landline phone or ask to borrow someone's phone to make an emergency call.

Seek Higher Ground: If you're in an area with poor reception, try moving to higher ground. Elevated locations may have a better chance of obtaining a cellular signal.

Utilize Emergency Signal Devices: If you're in a remote outdoor area or near water, opt for emergency signaling devices. These can include whistles, signal mirrors, flares, or brightly colored clothing to attract attention from potential rescuers.

Find a Safe Location: If you're unable to communicate for help, focus on finding a safe location to wait for assistance. Ensure you are protected from the elements, seek shelter if necessary, and conserve energy and resources while waiting for rescue.

Look for Alternative Routes: If you're stranded on the road, explore alternative routes or paths that may lead to areas with better reception or higher chances of encountering help.

lag Down Passing Vehicles: If you see vehicles passing by, make yourself visible and try to flag them down for assistance. Use hand signals or any available objects to attract attention.

While you can't always predict when you may lose reception, it's always handy to have an emergency kit prepared with things like a portable battery charger, an emergency whistle or essential survival items.

What to do if you get stuck in the woods

If you're planning a camping trip or an outdoor adventure with friends you'll want to ensure you're prepared for anything, like getting stuck in the woods. Before you head out though, you should always aim to go in groups and always tell someone where you're headed and when you're expected back. In the slim chance you get stuck in the woods, here are a few things to keep in mind:

1. Stop and Assess the Situation: Take a moment to stop walking and assess your surroundings. Make the most out of daylight. Look for any recognizable landmarks that can help you retrace your steps. If you're in a group, it's always best to stick together.

2. Stay Put and Avoid Panic: Unless you have a clear sense of direction and know how to find your way back, it's generally safer to stay in one place rather than wander aimlessly, especially if it's dark. This will make it easier for search parties to locate you.

3. Make Yourself Visible: Increase your visibility to potential searchers or rescuers by wearing bright-colored clothing or tying a brightly colored item to a tree. This will make it easier for others to spot you from a distance.

4. Signal for Help: Use any available means to signal for help. This can include shouting or yelling, blowing a whistle, or using a flashlight or mirror to reflect sunlight. Three short blasts on a whistle is a universal distress signal.

5. Build a Shelter: If you get stuck overnight or it's been a few days in the woods, it's important to build a shelter to protect yourself from the elements. Look for natural materials like branches, leaves, or moss to construct a simple shelter that provides insulation and keeps you dry.

6. Find a Water Source: Locate a nearby water source such as a stream or river. Never drink from stagnant pools of water as it could be filled with bacteria that could make you ill. Before you drink the water, you'll want to purify it through boiling or using water purification tablets if necessary.

7. Start a Fire: If you have the means and resources, start a fire. Fire can provide warmth, act as a signal, and help keep wildlife at bay. Make sure to select a safe location away from dry vegetation and keep the fire under control.

8. Make Noise: Make noise, such as clapping or banging on objects, to alert potential rescuers to your presence. This can help them locate you, especially if they are conducting a search in your area.

9. Stay Positive and Mentally Strong: It's important to stay positive and mentally strong during this challenging time. Keeping a positive mindset will help you think clearly and make better decisions.

10. If Possible, Follow Water or Go Uphill: If you decide to move from your current location, consider following a water source downhill or try to climb to higher ground. These actions can increase your chances of finding civilization or help.

What to do in a power outage?

Power outages can happen whether you live in a city or rural area. Is your home ready for one? You should aim to have non-perishable food items, water, flashlight and a first aid kit. Here's what to do next time the power is out.

Check the location of the outage: Look outside to see if your neighbors' homes are also without power. If the lights seem to be out on your block, contact your utility company to report the outage. If not, you might want to check your fuse box.

Keep your food cool: Keep refrigerator and freezer doors closed as much as possible to maintain the cold temperature. A well-insulated refrigerator can keep food cold for about four hours, while a full freezer can maintain its temperature for up to 48 hours (24 hours for a half-full freezer).

Find light: Keep flashlights, battery-powered lanterns, and extra batteries readily available. Avoid using candles, as they pose a fire hazard.

Unplug electronic devices: To protect your devices from power surges when the electricity is restored, unplug sensitive electronics such as computers, TVs, and gaming consoles.

Be cautious with generators: If you have a generator, follow the manufacturer's instructions and use it outdoors in a well-ventilated area. Do not operate a generator indoors, as it can produce dangerous carbon monoxide fumes.

Be ware of open flames Keep a close eye on candles, lanterns, or any other open flames you may be using. Ensure that all flames are extinguished before going to bed or leaving the room.

Help others: Check on elderly neighbors, friends, or family members who may require assistance during the outage, especially if they rely on medical equipment or have limited mobility.

Chapter 8: Social Skills

How to make friends

Making friends in your tweens and teens can be tricky especially if you've moved schools. While you may not find people you gel with right away, there are a few things you can do to improve your chances.

Explore Hobbies: At the core of the best friendships are people you share similar values with and you're likely to find them doing things you love. Look into joining classes or sports clubs, anything extracurricular activities you may be interested in.

Be Mindful of Your Body Language: Did you know that most communication is through body language? That said you'll want to be mindful or your posture. Stand up straight with confidence, and avoid crossing your arms and legs. Smile and make eye contact, this will make you more approachable.

Engage in Group Projects: Whether it's a school project or a community initiative, working together in a group setting provides an opportunity to collaborate, connect, and build friendships.

Volunteer: Participate in volunteer activities or community service projects. If you love the outdoors and nature, consider volunteering at a community garden. If you love animals, look into working at an animal shelter. Not only will you gain valuable work and life experience, you might also make a friend or two in your journey.

Get Social: It may seem daunting to attend social events when you don't have any friends but remember that there are probably people in the same scenario as you are. Work up the courage and attend school socials and dances.

Making friends takes time and effort. Don't be disheartened if you don't make friends right away. Be patient. It's better to have a handful of genuine friendships than a party of friends you only know on the surface.

Friendship Etiquette

To find and keep good friends, you need to be one. There are no hard rules when it comes to friendships but here's how you can be a good friend.

Listen: Be present when a friend is speaking. Whether it be a debrief about their day, problems with family or a personal issue, always take the time to listen. Ask questions, offer support, and show empathy. People appreciate being heard and understood. Remember that if a friend is telling you their problems, often they don't need a solution, they just want someone to listen.

Be Kind: It goes a long way to be kind. Treat others with respect, show support, and avoid engaging in gossip or negative behavior that could harm relationships.

Make an Effort: Once you've made new friends, you'll need to maintain them. Life gets busy but it's important to show up for your friends, especially when they need you the most. Good friends show up, even if it may be inconvenient.

Signs of a Healthy Relationship

You're likely to be interested in dating by now, what an exciting time! While some people may be attractive to you, it doesn't mean that you're meant to be together. A healthy relationship should uplift and bring out the best in you. Here's how to recognise if you're in a healthy relationship:

You Have Space to Grow: You and your partner spend quality time together but also spend time apart doing things you love.

There's Mutual Respect: They make you feel loved and appreciated. You always feel good about yourself, even in an argument.

You Can Be Yourself: You have space to be yourself and never feel you need to change who you are.

There's Trust: Trust is the foundation of a healthy relationship. Do you trust your partner with your fears, thoughts and feelings? Is it mutual?

You're Supported: A great partner is there for you, when times are great and when times aren't so good.
Keep in mind, even the best relationships can run its course. It's ok to say goodbye and move on if things don't work out.

Dealing with peer pressure

It can be tempting to do something all your classmates and friends are doing, even if it doesn't feel right for you. But always keep in mind that you have a choice. And if you want to opt out of doing something, the chances are you're in good company. Always trust your gut instincts, if it doesn't feel right, step away. Focus on knowing your own values and beliefs. The stronger they are, the easier it will be to say no to things that go against them.

If you're in a position where you feel pressured to do something your friends are doing, keep the following tips in mind:

Find Like-Minded People: Look for friends who respect and support your choices. Surrounding yourself with like-minded individuals who share your values can help limit the chances of being pressured into doing something you don't feel comfortable with.

Learn to Say No: Saying 'no' is a learned skill and one that most adults are still struggling to practice. Know that you are your number one priority and that it's ok to say no and put yourself first.

Suggest Another Activity: Offer alternative suggestions for things to do together that align with your values and interests.

Find a Mentor: If something doesn't sit well with you, speak to an adult. Mentors can offer guidance, advice, and support to help you navigate through challenging moments.

When in double, always trust your gut. You will find friends who accept you for who you are.

Avoiding gossip

Gossip is defined as conversation or chatter about a person who isn't present, often in a casual manner. Examples of gossip could be spreading a rumor, sharing a secret your friend told you in private, participating in social media with hateful comments, discussing the personal details of people's lives and commenting on another's body image.

You may not even notice you've engaged in gossip but before you participate in a conversation about another person, question if it brings value to your life or that individual's. Is the conversation helpful or productive? Most gossip is toxic even if the intent is otherwise.

The next time your friends engage in a topic about another friend, direct the conversation away from it. If friends are telling you about their concerns about a mutual friend, speak to the mutual friend instead directly. The issue with gossip is that it leaves a lot of room for secrecy and miscommunication. While talking about someone may bond you and another person, it's at the expense of someone else's being.

Think about the Intent: Consider the impact your words may have on others, and question what value they may bring.
Keep Secrets to Yourself: Friendships are built on trust. If a friend tells you a secret, you should do everything you can to keep it.

Change the Subject: You have the power to change the conversation. Steer the conversation towards shared interests or current events.

Take the Lead: Gossip can't continue unless there are people participating in it. Lead by example by opting out of engaging in gossip.

Practice Empathy: Put yourself in the shoes of the person being talked about. Consider how it would feel if you were in their position. Developing empathy can help you understand the potential harm that gossip can cause.

Surround yourself with friends who share your values and are committed to avoiding gossip. Choose friends who encourage and support positive behavior.

Stand Up to Bullies

Bullies can be found regardless of your age or where you live. The number one thing to remember when it comes to bullies is this:

You show people how you want to be treated

It may be hard to have empathy for them but bullies often have underlying issues that cause them to hurt others. They're fighting a battle too. That said, it does not excuse their behavior or take away your power from standing up to them. Bullying can come in all forms. Whether it be physical pharm, online trolling or name-calling, the behavior is not acceptable.

Next time you encounter a bully, be assertive. Firmly let me know that their behavior is making you uncomfortable and that you are walking away. If they persist, look to friends or a teacher/adult for support. Remember to put your safety first. If the bullying continues, keep a document of all the interactions. This could include screenshots containing hateful comments, emails and video evidence of the bullying. Share them with an adult so they are aware and can monitor their situation. If you are being bullied, the chances are there are others in the same scenario who may not be so brave. Don't be afraid to speak up.

Respecting Differences

While you and your friends are likely to share common interests and values, there will be times when you may have your differences. This could be cultural differences (e.g. language barriers or speaking with an accent), preference for a certain type of guy/girl in dating or it could be a difference in communication styles. It's important to understand that not everyone is exactly like you and it's a great thing. In fact, it's how we grow and learn. Embrace the differences you encounter and use them to enrich your life experience.

How to Handle Criticism

Knowing how to handle criticism is one of the best skills you can acquire. Though it sounds negative, there's a lot we can learn from a challenging conversation. Next time you receive criticism, try to take the emotion away from it. It's natural to feel defensive and explain your side of the story but it's more important to listen to the criticism and see if there's room for you to improve. For example, you may have received a C- in a paper you wrote. While you can speak to your teacher and justify why you should've received a B, you can also pause to reflect on any comments or feedback they may have left you. There's always something to learn from negative feedback. Use it to your advantage.

How to Make an Accept an Apology

Another essential life skill is knowing when to say sorry and how to accept an apology with grace. When you're in the wrong, our egos can get in the way of mending a relationship with a friend or family member. But if you get past it, reflect on your actions. Acknowledge where you may have been at fault and make an apology. A simple 'I'm sorry for hurting your feelings' is much more effective than an apology followed by an excuse like "I'm sorry I hurt your feelings but you did this, this and that…".

If someone apologizes to you, all you need to do is say thank you and move on. Just like that. There's no need to rehash what happened or make them feel worse when they already feel remorse. Learn from the experience and move on.

Chapter 9: Digital Literacy

People are scared to have a strong opinion because, with social media, everyone lives the life of a celebrity
— Yungblud

We're lucky to live in an age where Wi-Fi is easily accessible and we can connect with anyone around the world with a phone. But if your social life is centered around your phone, you're missing out.

It's great to chat with friends online over shared interests but there's nothing like sharing those interests in person and building a genuine connection over a hot chocolate of fresh juice. Hanging out with friends provides a sense of belonging and support you wouldn't get online. It teaches you about body language and reading non-verbal cues. And let's be real, an online hug emoji just isn't the same as a real cuddle.

Cyber safety

With the convenience of technology also comes with people who are ready to take advantage of it. Cybercrime is increasing and it's crucial to stay safe. This means keeping your identity, your passwords and your information safe. Here are a few tips for staying safe online:

Be Mindful of the Information You Share: Think about your social posts before you upload them. For example, if your parents are on holiday and you'll be alone at home, do you want strangers to know that?

Don't Share Personal Information: The person on the other end may seem friendly and you may feel like you've known them for a lifetime, but you never know who is behind the screen. If someone is requesting personal information from you, make sure you've met them in person first and that you trust them.

Take Care When Using Public Wi-Fi: Public Wi-Fi may be free but it also may come at a cost. Avoid logging in to access sensitive information using Wi-Fi in public places like the library, train station or airport.

Protect Your Passwords: Change your passwords often and avoid using the same password across multiple sites. If you feel overwhelmed by the number of passwords you need to keep, consider using a Password Manager tool like LastPass.

While social media can bring entertainment and keep you connected, it's important that your real-life connections are just as important. Don't forget to put down your phone and enjoy the life in front of you.

Conclusion

Wow, can you believe it? We've reached the end of this awesome book about life skills for teen and tween girls! We've talked about so many things—from taking care of your mental health to discovering your passion and purpose. It's been quite a journey, hasn't it? The journey to adulthood is exciting. We hope you enjoy it. Some final tips before you head off to live your best life:

Embrace YOU: You're awesome, just the way you are. Celebrate your unique quirks and personality. Comparison is the thief of joy. Focus on your own journey and strive for personal growth rather than trying to fit into what society expects you to be.

Life is One Big Lesson: I once heard someone say that if you're not learning, you're dying. Curiosity keeps you youthful. Don't be afraid to explore new ideas, hobbies and perspectives. Don't be too quick to listen and trust what you read and see. Make your own informed decisions.

Build resilience: Life can be tough, but you are too. The quickest way to learn is actually from setbacks and obstacles. Develop resilience by learning from failures, adapting to change, and bouncing back stronger. Remember to learn from your network of friends and family during challenging times.

Follow your passions: Discover what truly brings you joy and fulfillment and find ways to incorporate them into your life.

Now, it's time to put all of these skills into practice! It's important to remember that developing life skills is an ongoing process. You won't become an expert overnight, but with time and practice, you'll get better and better.

I encourage you to continue to develop and practice these skills. Make a conscious effort to apply what you've learned in your daily life. You'll be surprised at how much of a difference it can make.

Remember, it's okay to make mistakes. No one is perfect, and we all have things to learn. Don't be too hard on yourself if you slip up. Instead, use it as a learning opportunity and try again.

References

A Quote by Confucius. (n.d.-a). Www.goodreads.com. https://www.goodreads.com/quotes/184310-the-man-who-asks-a-question-is-a-fool-for

A Quote by Confucius. (n.d.-b). Www.goodreads.com. https://www.goodreads.com/quotes/8564694-choose-a-job-you-love-and-you-will-never-have

A Quote From Atlas Shrugged. (n.d.). Www.goodreads.com. Retrieved May 9, 2023, from https://www.goodreads.com/quotes/7215632-money-is-only-a-tool-it-will-take-you-wherever

American Heart Association. (2018, April 18). American Heart Association Recommendations for Physical Activity in Adults and Kids. Www.heart.org. https://www.heart.org/en/healthy-living/fitness/fitness-basics/aha-recs-for-physical-activity-in-adults

Ayala, E. E., Winseman, J. S., Johnsen, R. D., & Mason, H. R. C. (2018). U.S. Medical Students Who Engage in Self-Care Report Less Stress and Higher Quality of Life. BMC Medical Education, 18(1). https://doi.org/10.1186/s12909-018-1296-x

Brennan, D. (2021, March 29). How Does Mental Health Affect Physical Health? WebMD. https://www.webmd.com/mental-health/how-does-mental-health-affect-physical-health

CDC. (2020, September 10). Sleep in Middle and High School Students. CDC. https://www.cdc.gov/healthyschools/features/students-sleep.htm

Chien, A. L.-L. (n.d.). Sunscreen and Your Morning Routine. www.hopkinsmedicine.org. https://www.hopkinsmedicine.org/health/wellness-and-prevention/sunscreen-and-your-morning-routine

Cooper, C. B., Neufeld, E. V., Dolezal, B. A., & Martin, J. L. (2018). Sleep Deprivation and Obesity in Adults: A Brief Narrative Review. BMJ Open Sport & Exercise Medicine, 4(1), e000392. https://doi.org/10.1136/bmjsem-2018-000392

De Netto, P. M., Quek, K. F., & Golden, K. J. (2021). Communication, the Heart of a Relationship: Examining Capitalization, Accommodation, and Self-construal on Relationship Satisfaction. Frontiers in Psychology, 12. https://doi.org/10.3389/fpsyg.2021.767908

Don't Let Yesterday Take Up Too Much of Today. - Will Rogers. (n.d.). Www.quotespedia.org. Retrieved May 9, 2023, from https://www.quotespedia.org/authors/w/will-rogers/dont-let-yesterday-take-up-too-much-of-today-will-rogers/

Ehrenfeld, T. (2018). The Three Types of Stress. Psychology Today. https://www.psychologytoday.com/us/blog/open-gently/201812/the-three-types-stress

Firmager, S. (2021, February 2). Goal Setting: It is Said That 14% of People Who Set Goals are 10 Times More Successful. www.linkedin.com. https://www.linkedin.com/pulse/goal-setting-said-14-people-who-set-goals-10-times-more-alrashe-/

Fletcher, J. (2019, May 31). Why is Sleep Important? 9 Reasons for Getting a Good Night's Rest. Medical News Today. https://www.medicalnewstoday.com/articles/325353

Gavin, M. (2019, February). How Much Sleep Do I Need? (for teens). Kidshealth.org. https://kidshealth.org/en/teens/how-much-sleep.html

Good Habits Formed at Youth Make All the Difference. (2011, April 25). Philosiblog. https://philosiblog.com/2011/04/25/make-all-the-difference/

Hall, J. (2021, January 19). Average Stock Market Return. The Motley Fool. https://www.fool.com/investing/how-to-invest/stocks/average-stock-market-return/

Hammett, E. (2017, August 2). 1 in 3 Brits Not Confident Saving Lives With First Aid. Online First Aid. https://onlinefirstaid.com/1-in-3-brits-not-confident-saving-lives-with-first-aid/

Hanke, S. (2017, October 30). Are People Actually Listening to and Understanding What You Say? Here are 5 Signs to Watch. Entrepreneur. https://www.entrepreneur.com/leadership/are-people-actually-listening-to-and-understanding-what-you/301188

Huckle, B. (2019, August 28). The Importance of Communication Skills: 5 Research-Backed Benefits. Secondnature. https://www.secondnature.com.au/blog/importance-of-communication-in-business/

IANS. (2023, February 26). "It's So Hard to be a Teenager, Incredibly Difficult," says Hugh Jackman. Thenewsmen. https://thenewsmen.co.in/entertainment/its-so-hard-to-be-a-teenager-incredibly-difficult-says-hugh-jackman/100484

Khajeali, N., Ahmady, S., Kalantarion, M., Sharifi, F., & Yaseri, M. (2021). Relation Between Stress, Time Management, and Academic Achievement in Preclinical Medical Education: A Systematic Review and Meta-analysis. Journal of Education and Health Promotion, 10(1), 32. https://doi.org/10.4103/jehp.jehp_600_20

Lindberg, S. (2019, January 3). Eustress: The Good Stress. Healthline. https://www.healthline.com/health/eustress

Lonczak, H. (2020, September 3). What is Assertive Communication? 10 Real-life Examples. PositivePsychology.com. https://positivepsychology.com/assertive-communication/

Lusardi, A. (2019). Financial Literacy and the Need for Financial Education: Evidence and Implications. Swiss Journal of Economics and Statistics, 155(1). https://doi.org/10.1186/s41937-019-0027-5

Mayo Clinic Staff. (2020, August 18). Exercise and Stress: Get Moving to Manage Stress. Mayo Clinic. https://www.mayoclinic.org/healthy-lifestyle/stress-management/in-depth/exercise-and-stress/art-20044469

Mayo Clinic Staff. (2021, March 24). Stress Management. Mayo Clinic. https://www.mayoclinic.org/healthy-lifestyle/stress-management/in-depth/stress-symptoms/art-20050987

Mirfattah, S. (2017, December 12). Conflict Resolution is First Mindset Then Skill Set. www.linkedin.com. https://www.linkedin.com/pulse/conflict-resolution-first-mindset-skill-set-saeed-mirfattah-m-a-/

Naidoo, U. (2022, May 14). A Harvard Nutritionist and Brain Expert Avoids These 5 Types of Foods That Can Make You "Tired and Stressed." CNBC. https://www.cnbc.com/2022/05/14/harvard-nutritionist-and-brain-expert-avoids-these-foods-that-make-you-tired-and-stressed.html

National Institute on Drug Abuse. (2020, July). Addiction and Health. National Institute on Drug Abuse. https://nida.nih.gov/publications/drugs-brains-behavior-science-addiction/addiction-health

Paruthi, S., Brooks, L. J., D'Ambrosio, C., Hall, W. A., Kotagal, S., Lloyd, R. M., Malow, B. A., Maski, K., Nichols, C., Quan, S. F., Rosen, C. L., Troester, M. M., & Wise, M. S. (2016). Consensus Statement of the American Academy of Sleep Medicine on the Recommended Amount of Sleep for Healthy Children: Methodology and Discussion. Journal of Clinical Sleep Medicine, 12(11), 1549–1561. https://doi.org/10.5664/jcsm.6288

Ryu, S., & Fan, L. (2022). The Relationship Between Financial Worries and Psychological Distress Among U.S. Adults. Journal of Family and Economic Issues, 44(1). https://doi.org/10.1007/s10834-022-09820-9

Schawbel, D. (2016, April 5). Arianna Huffington Shares How Sleep Can Make Leaders More Productive. Forbes. https://www.forbes.com/sites/danschawbel/2016/04/05/arianna-huffington-how-sleep-can-make-leaders-more-productive/?sh=24e71fbf52b8

SDSU News Team. (n.d.). Will Spending Money Make You Happy? Newscenter.sdsu.edu. Retrieved May 9, 2023, from https://newscenter.sdsu.edu/sdsu_newscenter/news_story.aspx?sid=78687

Sexually Transmitted Infections in Teens. (2019). Stanfordchildrens.org. https://www.stanfordchildrens.org/en/topic/default?id=sexually-transmitted-diseases-in-adolescents-90-P01654

60+ Self-Care Quotes to Remind You to Take Care of Yourself. (2023, March 13). The Honest Consumer. https://www.thehonestconsumer.com/blog/self-care-quotes

Škabar, A. (2019, July 15). "Communication - The Human Connection - Is the Key to Personal and Career Success". Www.linkedin.com. https://www.linkedin.com/pulse/communication-human-connection-key-personal-career-success-%C5%A1kabar/

Souders, B. (2019, April 9). 100+ Happiness Activities, Exercises, and Tools for Groups and Adults. PositivePsychology.com. https://positivepsychology.com/happiness-activities-exercises-tools/

Spence, J. (2020, February 18). Non-Verbal Communication: How Body Language & Non-verbal Cues are Key. Lifesize. https://www.lifesize.com/blog/speaking-without-words/

Tao, W., Zhao, D., Yue, H., Horton, I., Tian, X., Xu, Z., & Sun, H.-J. (2022). The Influence of Growth Mindset on the Mental Health and Life Events of College Students. Frontiers in Psychology, 13. https://doi.org/10.3389/fpsyg.2022.821206

UV Radiation. (2019, June). The Skin Cancer Foundation. https://www.skincancer.org/risk-factors/uv-radiation/

What is Goal-Setting Theory? (2013, March 5). GoStrengths! https://gostrengths.com/what-is-goal-setting-theory/

White, A. (2020, January 13). Alaskans Carry the Highest Credit Card Balance—Here's the Average Credit Card Balance in Every State. CNBC. https://www.cnbc.com/select/average-credit-card-balance-by-state/

www.ingramcontent.com/pod-product-compliance
Lightning Source LLC
Chambersburg PA
CBHW051541010526
44107CB00064B/2804